THE POWERHOUSE MX NATIONS

USA, Belgium, UK, Netherlands, France, and Germany

Bryan
Stealey

x1000r/min

CRABTREE PUBLISHING COMPANY
www.crabtreebooks.com

Crabtree Publishing Company

www.crabtreebooks.com

Coordinating editor: Chester Fisher
Series and project editor: Shoreline Publishing Group LLC
Author: Bryan Stealey
Series Consultant: Bryan Stealey
Project Manager: Kavita Lad
Art direction: Rahul Dhiman
Design: Ranjan Singh
Cover Design: Chhaya Sajwan
Photo research: Akansha Srivastava
EditorS: Adrianna Morganelli, Mike Hodge

Acknowledgments

The publishers would like to thanks the following for permission to reproduce photographs:

p4: Paul Buckley; p5: Simon Cudby; p6: Simon Cudby;
p7: Simon Cudby (all); p8: Hulton-Deutsch Collection/CORBIS;
p9: Terry Good Collection (top); p9: Racer X Archive (bottom);
p10: Simon Cudby; p11: Still MX Motocross Photography;
p12: Terry Good Collection; p13: Terry Good Collection (top);
p13: Hakan ERIKSSON (bottom); p14: Terry Good Collection;
p15: Terry Good Collection (all); p16: Randy Petree (top right);
p16: Simon Cudby (bottom left); p17: Paul Webb Photography (top);
p17: Randy Petree (bottom); p18: Simon Cudby; p19: Simon Cudby (all);
p20: Randy Petree; p21: Randy Petree (top); p21: Simon Cudby;
p22: Simon Cudby (all); p23: Simon Cudby; p24: Motoverte;
p25: Jerome Prevost/TempSport/Corbis (left); p25: Motoverte (right);
p26: Simon Cudby; p27: Simon Cudby (all); p28: Simon Cudby;
p29: Simon Cudby; p30: Simon Cudby; p31: Vince Bucci/Getty Images (top);
p31: ASSOCIATED PRESS (bottom)

Cover and title page image provided by REUTERS/Thierry Roge

Library and Archives Canada Cataloguing in Publication

Stealey, Bryan
    The powerhouse MX nations / Bryan Stealey.

(MXplosion!)
Includes index.
ISBN 978-0-7787-3990-6 (bound).--ISBN 978-0-7787-4003-2 (pbk.)

    1. Motocross--History--Juvenile literature. I. Title. II. Series.

GV1060.12.S74 2008   j796.7'56   C2008-901522-3

Library of Congress Cataloging-in-Publication Data

Stealey, Bryan.
    The powerhouse MX nations / Bryan Stealey.
        p. cm. -- (MXplosion!)
    Includes index.
    ISBN-13: 978-0-7787-4003-2 (pbk. : alk. paper)
    ISBN-10: 0-7787-4003-X (pbk. : alk. paper)
    ISBN-13: 978-0-7787-3990-6 (reinforced library binding : alk. paper)
    ISBN-10: 0-7787-3990-2 (reinforced library binding : alk. paper)
    1. Motocross--History--Juvenile literature. I. Title.
GV1060.12.S74 2008
796.7'56--dc22
                                        2008008950

Crabtree Publishing Company

Published in Canada
Crabtree Publishing
616 Welland Ave.
St. Catharines, ON
L2M 5V6

Published in the United States
Crabtree Publishing
PMB16A
350 Fifth Ave., Suite 3308
New York, NY 10118

Published in the United Kingdom
Crabtree Publishing
White Cross Mills
High Town, Lancaster
LA1 4XS

Published in Australia
Crabtree Publishing
386 Mt. Alexander Rd.
Ascot Vale (Melbourne)
VIC 3032

Contents

An International Affair   4

The First Kings of Motocross   8

The Swedes and Speed   12

The Nation of Moto   16

U.S.A. All the Way   20

The French Fly   24

Thunder from Down Under   28

Glossary and Index   32

An International Affair

Motocross racing is an international sport. Competitors line up on motocross tracks all over the world. While most nations have fast riders, there are some that have become powerhouse nations of the sport. To be considered a powerhouse, a nation's riders must do well in the world's most important races.

The Top Two Series

Since the 1950s, the Europe-based World Championships, or Grands Prix, have helped determine the fastest racers in the world. Riders could stay in their home countries to prove they were the best at home, but if they wanted to be the best in the world, they had to race in the World Championships. This series is still going strong in Europe and elsewhere. However, many consider the professional tours in the United States to be the most competitive. While top American riders rarely go to Europe to compete in the World Championships, the best riders from all over the world come to the U.S.A. to race. The two American series that top professionals compete in are the **AMA** Motocross Championships and the AMA Supercross Series. All three of these international series are extremely important in determining the powerhouse nations of motocross. But there's one other event that must be considered when talking about the strongest nations in the sport: the Motocross of Nations.

Motocross is a sport filled with patriotism, and flags can be seen flying at international events.

The Olympics of Motocross

Motocross isn't a team sport, right? That's not always true. Competitors usually line up to race against every other rider on the track, and the first person to cross the finish line is the winner. But back in 1947, the national motorcycle federation of the Netherlands decided to try something new. They wanted to see what would happen if the best riders in each country battled one another in a team format. Both Great Britain and Belgium called on their five fastest riders to travel to the Netherlands to compete against the best of the Dutch. The race was run normally, but each rider's times were combined with his countrymen's. The team with the lowest overall time could say that they were the fastest country in motocross. Great Britain's narrow victory over Belgium meant that they were the first country to win the Motocross des Nations.

Name Changes

Throughout the history of motocross, some important names have changed. The Motocross des Nations, for example, is now called the Motocross of Nations (MXoN). Also, many racing-class names have changed. In the World Championships, what used to be called the 250cc, 125cc, and 500cc classes are now the MX1, MX2, and MX3 classes. In U.S. racing, the classes used to be 125cc and 250cc. Now they are called the Lites class and the Supercross or Motocross class.

The 17-race AMA Supercross Series is the biggest racing series for dirt bikes in the world.

Let it Grow

While the first event was **modest** in size, the second Motocross des Nations was not! More than 30,000 fans crowded around the track in La Fraineuse, Belgium, to cheer on their nations' riders, and motocross fans have been doing that ever since. Countries from all over the world have sent their best riders to the annual "Olympics of Motocross" to try to prove they are the fastest. Fans often follow their teams, wearing funny costumes and body paint to show their support. Some countries, like England, Belgium, and the United States, have won the event many times. Others, like Italy, France, and Czechoslovakia (now the Czech Republic), have only won once or twice. Most countries have never won. It's no easy feat to beat the world's best and take home the biggest award in motocross: the Peter Chamberlain Trophy. The countries who field a strong enough team to accomplish this task have a lot to brag about.

The Motocross of Nations Now

It's been more than 60 years since the first international showdown, and the world's biggest race is still a lot like it used to be. But there have been some changes, too. Rules have been updated as the sport has grown. Classes have changed, allowing racers to choose different motorcycles than in the past. Crowds at the big events have gotten bigger and rowdier. Countries that used to dominate these international events have fallen aside, and new nations have stepped up to take their place. New riders emerge as stars on the world scene, too. But one thing that hasn't changed is the importance of finding a way to win the **prestigious** race. It's hard for a country to be considered a powerhouse nation if they don't win the Motocross of Nations.

Motocross of Nations Wins by Country

USA	18
Great Britain	16
Belgium	14
Sweden	7
Italy	2
U.S.S.R.	2
Czechoslovakia	1
France	1

The Peter Chamberlain Trophy is one of the most important prizes in motocross.

These French fans show their national pride with face paint and patriotic clothing.

The First Kings of Motocross

The first country to dominate motocross was Great Britain, where the sport was invented. More than 20 years after the English held the first official off-road race, they were still just getting started.

The Earliest Heroes

Great Britain proved that they were the real deal when they won the first Motocross des Nations in 1947. That year, five young Englishmen headed to the Netherlands with nothing on their minds but winning. Bill Nicholson, Fred Rist, and Ray Scovell all rode English-made BSA motorcycles. Jack Stocker and Bob Ray were both on Ariels, which were also made in Great Britain. With so many nice motorcycles being produced on the island nation, it's no wonder there were so many fast riders. So many, in fact, that Great Britain

managed to win the Motocross des Nations 14 more times in the next 20 years. The first rider to ever race on more than one winning Motocross des Nations team was Englishman Harold Lines. In 1949 and 1950, the popular speedster helped his nation take the trophy aboard an Ariel 350. In the following years, Geoff Ward would help Great Britain to four wins. They were some of the best-known motorcyclists in the world, winning race after race in their home country and others.

Off-road motorcycle riding and racing have been huge in Great Britain since the first scrambles race there in 1924.

A Man Named Smith

Of all the amazing English motocross racers, Jeff Smith was probably the best. He grew up during World War II in Colne, England, watching his father ride motorcycles. Imagine how excited he must have been when his dad bought him his own motorcycle! It was a Triumph, but because gasoline was **scarce**, he was only allowed to ride a little at a time. After the war, his father bought him a 125cc two-stroke BSA motorcycle, and Smith began riding in local events. (Motocross engines are either two-strokes or four-strokes, which describes the action of the engines as they are running). He found that he had a natural ability on his bike, and he soon began winning different kinds of motorcycle competitions. By 1952, when he was winning motocross races all over on a Norton motorcycle, he was hired by the company. His career as a professional motocross racer was just beginning. By the time it was over, nearly 20 years later, he was one of the most successful racers ever. Smith won two World Championships and nine British championships. He was also a member of six winning Motocross des Nations teams.

Jeff Smith (above) was one of the most successful early English motocross racers.

In addition to great racers, Great Britain produced many of the best motocross machines in the 1950s and 1960s. This Rickman Metisse (below) signaled a revolutionary change in manufacturing.

Fall From Grace

One of the problems with being the best in the world is that the only way to go is down. Great Britain managed to rule the motocross world for decades, but it wouldn't last forever. The last Motocross des Nations event that the English won was in 1967. Since then, the country has been shut out at the international event. There have been moments of glory, however. Graham Noyce won the 1979 500cc World Championship on a Honda. Two years later, Neil Hudson managed to win the 250cc World Championship on his Yamaha. The most recent world champion from England was the popular James Dobb. He won the title in the 125cc class in 2001. He's also one of the few English riders to win a professional AMA race in the United States, at the famous Southwick racetrack. But perhaps the last truly great motocrosser from Great Britain was a man named David Thorpe.

Thorpy!

David Thorpe almost didn't race motocross. He was an excellent soccer player—so good that he was offered a contract to play the team sport professionally. Fortunately for English racing fans, he chose motocross. In 1985, he put the country back on the map. That's the year he won his first 500cc World Championship. He successfully defended his title in 1986, and then won a third World Championship in 1989. All of those victories were on a Honda. English fans rejoiced! In 1990, he moved to a Kawasaki motorcycle that couldn't compete with the Hondas. After a few more years of racing, he retired as a professional. He then spent his time helping other racers from his country achieve success.

James Dobb (right) is one of the most successful and popular English racers in recent history.

Tommy Searle (above) is England's best chance at finding success again on the world stage.

The Next Big Thing?

Times have been tough for English motocross lately — but there's hope. A young man named Tommy Searle has shown that he can compete with the world's fastest! He finished in second place in the MX2 class in the 2007 World Championships. Who knows how far this shooting star will go?

The British Nationals

Many countries have their own thriving professional circuits, and England is no exception. In fact, the British Nationals are considered among the more important series in all of Europe. Riders from all over the continent—and also from the United States—compete in this exciting series. Many of them hope they will do well enough to get some attention from the World Championships team managers. For other racers, just making it to the British Nationals is a dream come true.

The Swedes and Speed

Early Swedish motocrossers were among the most stylish racers in the world. They were also among the fastest. In fact, Sweden's 16 world championships rank second on the all-time list.

The Nordic Nightmares

Bill Nilsson. Sten Lundin. Rolf Tibblin. Torsten Hallman. Bengt Aberg. In the early days of European motocross, these Swedish riders struck fear into the hearts of competitors across the continent. When the World Championships were created in Europe in 1957, Sweden wasted no time in showing other countries who was boss. Bill Nilsson, on an AJS dirt bike, won the championship that year. In fact, from 1955 to 1974, Sweden seemed to have more success than any other nation. During that time, riders from the **Nordic** country won seven Motocross des Nations trophies and 20 World Championships! The Swedish racers were known for their acrobatic styles and animal-like **stamina**. It seemed easy for them to wrestle heavy four-strokes around some of the roughest courses in the world. Later, when many competitors were on lighter two-stroke dirt bikes, the Swedes could ride those, too. It seemed like nothing could stop these iron men from dominating the sport forever.

Sweden not only produced dominant racers, they also produced amazing motorcycles. Husqvarna is one of the most important brands *in the history of motocross.*

12

Mean Machines

Fast racing wasn't the only thing that the Swedes did well in motocross. They also made fast dirt bikes. Many of the championships won during the glory years were aboard Swedish motorcycles. Monarks and Husabergs were both popular motorcycles, not only with professional racers, but also with more **casual** riders. But the Swedish bike that made the biggest impact on motocross was easily the Husqvarna. In fact, most of the championships won by these riders were thanks to their trusty "Husky" dirt bikes. Later, these Husqvarnas would also bring big changes to motocross in the United States.

Husky Tools

Motocrossers think of dirt bikes when they hear the name Husqvarna, but the company also makes chain saws, lawn mowers, and other motorized tools.

(right) Husqvarna didn't limit their participation to motocross. This team competed in an enduro race in Baja, Mexico, in 1969. A bike has to be strong to last for hundreds of miles in the desert.

(left) Bill Nilsson was one of Sweden's best racers, helping his country win three early Motocross des Nations events. He might not look happy in this picture, but that's because he's so intent on going fast.

Edison and the Flying Circus

The Husqvarna motorcycle changed motocross in the United States forever. In the 1960s, an American businessman named Edison Dye went to Europe and saw Sweden's motocross superstars at their best. He'd never seen anyone in the U.S.A. do what these guys did on their powerful, lightweight Huskys. He knew that he would be able to sell the bikes back home, so he made a deal with Husqvarna to import them into North America. At first, the motorcycles didn't sell very well, so Dye decided to bring a Swede over to demonstrate how they could be ridden. He hired four-time World Champion Torsten Hallman, who was excited to have the opportunity to race in the United States. When he got there, he found that he could easily beat the best riders in America. The fans were stunned. They had never seen anybody ride a motorcycle like Hallman did. Later, Dye brought other European stars over to race the Husqvarnas. The plan worked, and Huskys started selling like hotcakes. This "Flying Circus" of pure talent also showed Americans that they had a long way to go to become a powerhouse nation of motocross.

The 1970 Husqvarna tour exposed the Swedish brand to thousands of new riders.

All Good Things Must End

While Sweden had plenty of motocross success in the 1950s, 1960s, and early 1970s, it didn't last forever. Other countries emerged to take their place atop the world stage. Though the Swedes kept riding, eventually they slipped from power and struggled to win championships. In fact, Hakan Carlqvist (1983) and Marcus Hansson (1994) are the only Swedes who have won World Championships in the last 30 years. Even the mighty Husqvarna is no longer a major threat on the world stage.

Four-time World Champion Torsten Hallman (above) showed Americans how fast a motocross bike could be ridden.

Hallman manhandles his light Husqvarna around a Belgian racetrack.

What a Win!

Nobody races Husqvarnas professionally in U.S. motocross anymore, but that hasn't always been the case. At the turn of this century, Husqvarna actually had their own race team on the AMA circuit. In 2001, the team had its best moment when Travis Preston won a supercross race on a Husky 125. Too bad the brand had been bought by an Italian company years before.

The Nation of Moto

With 14 Motocross des Nations wins and 51 World Championships, Belgium may be the greatest nation in the history of motocross. That's no surprise, considering that most of the people who live there seem to be crazy about the sport.

The Sport of the People

Along with soccer, motocross is one of the most popular sports in Belgium. Newspapers and television programs cover Belgian motocross racers' **heroic** victories. Top Belgian racers are treated like rock stars when they're spotted in public places, and people chase them for their autographs. This is probably because racers from the nation have a long history of dominance in the sport. In fact, no other country in the world has achieved the amount of success in World Championship motocross that Belgium has. Many of these great wins were thanks to two of the best racers the world has ever seen. One is known as "The Man," and the other is called "The King."

The Man

Roger "The Man" DeCoster is a living legend. In his racing days, he was feared by everyone on the track. During his career in Europe, he won five 500cc World Championships. This included a record 36 wins in the class. He also helped his country win six Motocross des Nations titles. He even found success in the United States, where he won four Trans-AMA Motocross Championships. His amazing skill on the bike helped "The Man" teach many American racers how to ride like the faster European models. While racers may have been afraid of him, fans loved him and his charming ways. After a race, he could often be found smiling coolly at the top of the **podium**.

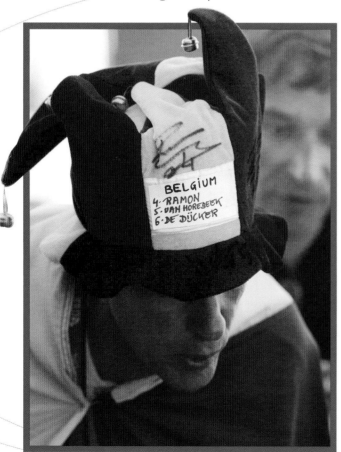

A fan at the 2007 Motocross of Nations cheers on his beloved Belgians with yet another funny hat.

16

When he finally retired, DeCoster moved to the United States, where he worked for some of the top teams on the pro tour. DeCoster is now the manager for Team Suzuki. He was Ricky Carmichael's boss in the last years of the American's amazing career. Since he's been in the U.S.A., DeCoster has almost always been the team manager for the American Motocross of Nations squad. He's led Team U.S.A. to 17 of its 18 MXoN wins. It's no wonder Roger DeCoster is known as "The Man."

Belgian legend Roger DeCoster leads Vic Allen at a 1973 Trans-AMA race in the United States.

Known as "The Man," DeCoster raced all over the world, including this Copetown 500cc GP in Canada, in 1975.

The King s Reign

When it comes to European motocross racers, Belgium's Stefan "The King" Everts is the greatest of all time. Some fans even think he was better than American Ricky Carmichael. He grew up watching his father, Harry, win four World Championships. Stefan started riding at an early age, and everyone around him knew he was going to be good. He lived up to that expectation when he started racing professionally. At one time or another, he raced in every class of World Championship motocross, and won titles in all of them. His ten championships and 101 wins are both records that may never be broken in European motocross. He even led Team Belgium to a victory over Ricky Carmichael and his teammates at the 2004 Motocross of Nations. But even though he was so good at racing, Stefan had many other interests during his career. He loves playing the drums, and even had a hit song on the Belgian charts called "I Am the Greatest!" When he walks down the street, the Belgian people whisper and look at him like he is a real king. He's one of the most popular athletes the country has ever known. After retiring in 2006, Stefan took a job as the race director for KTM motorcycle's professional team. He now helps young riders work hard to win World Championships of their own.

The greatest European racer of all-time, Belgian's Stefan Everts signs autographs for fans.

The Streak

When Belgian Steve Ramon won the MX1 World Championship in 2007, his countrymen cheered. That was the fifth year in a row that a Belgian motocrosser had won the important title. (Stefan Everts won the four years before). In 2008, Ramon will be back to try to keep his country's streak alive. Can he make it six years in a row?

Belgian's Steve Ramon is the reigning MX1 World Champion. He hopes to repeat the accomplishment in 2008.

Not only was Everts fast on a motocross bike, but his smooth style is legendary the world over.

Order Up!

If you go to a race in Belgium, what kind of food do you think you'll find to eat? Belgian waffles, of course. Fans wait in long lines to order the delicious snacks in between races. If the line is too long, they may decide to get French fries instead — only the Belgians eat them with mayonnaise instead of ketchup.

U.S.A. All the Way

Americans started racing motocross later than most European countries did. By the time they finally caught on, it wasn't long before nobody could stop them. The U.S.A. has been one of motocross's powerhouse nations ever since.

Hurricane Warning

When the 1970s began, motocross was just starting to get popular in the United States. Many colorful characters made up the professional tour. When the Europeans came over to race, American riders realized they had some catching up to do. There were various series, and eventually the AMA Motocross Championships became the most important in the country. American riders started to ride much faster. When the country was introduced to a brash young rider named Bob "Hurricane" Hannah, they never would have guessed that he'd become a legend.

When he first turned pro, most people had never heard of him. He rode well and had strong finishes in the 125cc class, but a Honda rider named Marty Smith was the big dog in the class. Hannah became a star in 1976 when he surprised everyone by beating Smith in the first race of the year. That year, he won five of eight races on his way to his first championship—and it wouldn't be his last. In the coming years, he would win seven AMA Motocross Championships and three AMA Supercross Championships. He is widely considered the first supercross superstar.

Marty Smith (9), Bob Hannah (5), and more, soon after the start of a 1977 Trans-AMA race.

Near the end of his career, Hannah became very interested in flying. After retiring from motocross, he decided to take up airplane racing. He now lives in Idaho, where he owns an airplane-sales business.

Indoor MX

The most popular form of dirt-bike racing in the world is supercross. While some other countries do have supercross races, nothing compares to the AMA Supercross Series. These races are held inside America's biggest sports stadiums, and tens of thousands of people come out to watch. The events are raced by many of the same riders who compete in AMA motocross. Supercross racing involves motorcycles riding on man-made dirt tracks. The races feature lots of jumping, spectacular crashes, and plenty of excitement. The top racers in AMA Supercross have won millions in prize money and **endorsements**.

Bob Hannah was the first supercross star, and he was extremely fast in outdoor motocross, too. Here he's flying around a turn in 1977.

Leading the Pack

When it comes to the Motocross of Nations, nobody has more wins than Team USA. They didn't get their first victory until 1981, but then they won 13 in a row! As of 2007, the American team has 18 MXoN victories, which is two more than motocross powerhouse nation Great Britain.

Team Suzuki's Ryan Dungey shows off while winning an AMA Supercross race in 2007. Motocross has come a long way in the U.S.A.

21

It s Showtime!

Bob Hannah may have been the first supercross superstar, but he wasn't the biggest. That honor goes to the best supercross racer of all time, Jeremy McGrath. Nicknamed "Showtime" for his flashiness, McGrath may be the most popular American racer ever. Many professionals started riding dirt bikes as small children, but not Jeremy. He spent his childhood on BMX bikes instead (these are bicycles that are pedaled over short, rough dirt tracks). But when he became a teenager, he decided he wanted to try a bike with a motor. Jeremy was a natural, and he began winning races almost immediately. He worked his way to the pro ranks, and before long, he was beating the best riders in the world. By the time his career was over, McGrath's records were almost unbelievable. His 72 supercross wins and seven supercross championships are records that will last a very long time. While supercross was his specialty, Jeremy was also a great motocross racer. He won one championship and numerous races in the AMA Motocross Championships. After he retired from full-time racing, McGrath tried other forms of motorcycle riding. He even won a gold medal in the 2004 X Games, in the Moto X Step-Up competition. Jeremy McGrath did as much for motocross and supercross in the U.S.A. as anyone ever has.

Jeremy McGrath was known as "Showtime" for his wild style. But he was known as "The King" for his outright dominance.

McGrath shows that perfect style as he gets some major air above a California track.

Ricky's the G.O.A.T.

Unlike Jeremy McGrath, Ricky Carmichael started racing motocross at a very early age—and he was always the best. As he rose through the ranks from amateur to professional, he dominated every class. The only time Ricky Carmichael really had trouble was when he moved to the 250cc class of AMA Supercross. There, he had a **tendency** to crash a lot, sometimes making others crash. At first, many fans didn't like him and would boo loudly from the stands. But Carmichael worked harder than all of the other racers, and soon he figured out how to win Supercross-class championships, as well. As he matured, the fans started to respect him, and the booing stopped. But the winning didn't. Before Carmichael came along, many professionals lived like rock stars. Some were known for loving wild parties. Carmichael instead spent his time training to win. This forced other riders to get more serious, just so they would have a chance to beat him. But most wins went to Carmichael. When he retired in 2007, he had 150 combined AMA motocross and supercross wins, plus 15 championships. That's why he's called the G.O.A.T.: Greatest Of All Time. Now Ricky is trying to find the same kind of success as a stock-car racer.

Ricky Carmichael has won more combined motocross and supercross races than anybody else in the history of the sport.

Next Big Things

McGrath and Carmichael are retired, but there are still superstars in American racing. James Stewart has a real chance to break some records, and Lites racer Ryan Villopoto appears to be at the beginning of a remarkable career, as well.

The French Fly

If you look at the list of Motocross of Nations winners, it might not seem like France was ever a powerhouse nation of the sport. But in the last twenty years, they've produced many great racers.

Frenchman Jacky Vimond may be on the ground here, but he was usually flying near the front of the pack.

Crazy 80s

The Americans began to find their motocross groove in the 1970s, and the same happened to the French in the late 1980s. The country didn't record its first World Championship until Jacky Vimond won the 250cc title in 1986. That accomplishment seemed to open the door for other French riders to succeed in international motocross. Jean-Michel Bayle followed with World Championships in the 125cc class in 1988 and 250cc class in 1989. These huge wins helped motocross become a national **pastime** in France.

The Great JMB

Jean-Michel Bayle may have been the best all-around French motorcycle racer ever. After winning the World Championships, "JMB" decided to move across the ocean to race against the Americans. In 1991, he did what nobody thought was possible: he won all three major American titles in the same year. First, he won the 250cc AMA Supercross Series title. That by itself was enough to surprise American fans. But what he did next really blew everyone away. Bayle raced in both major motocross classes that summer and won both championships. It was a remarkable feat that nobody before him had accomplished. The next year, however, Bayle's heart was no longer in motocross. After struggling on the American circuit in 1992, JMB retired from motocross and started a successful career in motorcycle road racing. He still competes in different forms of motorcycle and automobile racing. In fact, he's one of Europe's top rally-car racers. This is the same type of automobile that American superstar Travis Pastrana currently races. Don't be surprised if you see the two legends of motocross competing against each other on four wheels at the 2008 Summer X Games.

Moto-Cross

When the British invented motocross in the 1920s, they called it "scrambles," but the sport soon made its way to France. It wasn't long until the French came up with another name for the thrilling sport. They renamed it "moto-cross," which was a combination of the words "motorcycle" and "cross-country." Obviously, the name stuck!

Jean-Michel Bayle is France's best racer ever. Not only did he win in Europe, but he dominated the U.S.A.

Vimond shows his stuff in a race with the world's fastest riders.

French Invasion

Jean-Michel Bayle's success in America set off a wave of French riders trying to win in the States as well. They wanted to experience the glory that JMB had found. The next French rider to win a championship in the USA was Mickael Pichon. He was a supercross **specialist**, and he managed to win AMA 125cc Supercross Championships in 1995 and 1996. Frenchman Stephane Roncada, following Pichon's trail, repeated that feat in 2000. More and more French racers followed. Two-time World Champion Sebastien Tortelli came over for one supercross race in 1998, and he surprised everyone by winning. The next year, he moved to the U.S.A. to race full-time. Frenchman David Vuillemin headed to the United States in 2000 and is still racing the series today. He's won three Supercross-class races. There are even more French riders currently racing in America, and there are more still planning on making the move in the future.

The Bercy Supercross, in Paris, is one of the most exciting races in the world.

The Next Import

Christophe Pourcel won an MX2 title on the World Championship tour in 2006. He then announced his plan to come to the U.S. to race full-time in the AMA Supercross series in 2008. Things were looking very good for this young French superstar when he signed a deal to race for the powerful Pro Circuit Kawasaki team. In 2007, he raced a couple of AMA Lites Supercross Series races, winning one of them. All of the stars seemed to line up, and Americans expected Pourcel to challenge for a championship as the 2008 season of indoor races began. But an injury has Pourcel focusing on getting well instead of getting faster. If the youngster can get healthy again, he should be a force in American supercross for years to come.

David Vuillemin, who still competes on the U.S. tours, is one of France's best-ever racers.

The Bercy Supercross

Supercross isn't nearly as big in most of Europe as it in the U.S.A., but it's big in France. The biggest French race by far is the Bercy Supercross race. Every November, many of the fastest supercross riders in the world go to Paris, France, to compete in this event. The fans are always very rowdy, with smoke machines and laser shows making them even more excited. Unlike most races, this one lasts three nights. The person who has the best combined finishes after the weekend is crowned the winner.

Christophe Pourcel (377) hopes to be the next Frenchman to find fame, fortune, and glory on the American circuit.

Thunder from Down Under

The newest powerhouse nations in the world of motocross and supercross are Australia and New Zealand. While they're both very far from the rest of the motocrossing world, they're very close to each other. And they have lots of fast racers.

Racing Round the World

Motocross racing is considered a major sport in Australia. The country has a lot of land, and that makes finding places to ride pretty easy. Because of this, there are also a lot of fast racers there. Their close neighbor, New Zealand, also produces many great racers. The best riders from each country often race against each other at different tracks. But lately, the very best racers from each country have been coming to the United States to compete professionally. It all seemed to start with a rider named Chad Reed, who moved to the U.S.A. in 2002. After spending a year racing in Europe, he wanted to fulfill his dream of coming to America. He quickly became a superstar and a champion, and many others have tried to follow in his footsteps.

Chad Reed is easily one of the best racers in the world, and he has a Supercross-class Championship to prove it.

Reed All About It

Chad Reed had his first taste of big-time success when he won the Australian Supercross Championship in 2000. He was then offered a ride by Factory Kawasaki in the World Championships in 2001. He had a very good year, winning one race and finishing the 125cc class in second place. Not bad for a rookie. But Reed really wanted to be in America, and the next year he moved to the U.S.A. to compete in the 125cc class. He won five out of seven supercross races that year, easily winning the AMA Eastern Regional Championship. In 2004, he won the most important championship in dirt-bike racing: the 250cc AMA Supercross Championship. Today, he is one of the best racers in the world. He finishes on the **podium** in almost every race he enters. Reed no longer competes in many professional motocross races, choosing instead to focus on supercross. But he's extremely fast no matter what kind of track he's on.

While most racers ride both indoors and out, Reed prefers to focus on stadium racing.

New Zealand's Ben Townley is another fast racer from down under who's come to the U.S.A. and won a championship.

The New Zealanders

Considering how small New Zealand is, it's amazing how many great racers come from there. The best known in the United States is Ben Townley. The likeable young rider started his career in Europe, winning the 125cc World Championship in 2004. In 2006, he suffered an injury and was unable to compete. But in 2007, he lived up to his potential and won the AMA Eastern Regional Supercross Lites Championship. Another well known New Zealander is Josh Coppins. He's widely considered to be the fastest racer in the World Championships. He was expected to win the MX1 class in 2007. Unfortunately, he hurt himself while holding a huge points lead. He wasn't able to finish the season, and he lost the title.

Maddo the Madman

Some motocross racers find that they can make a better living by not racing their motorcycles. Australian Robbie Maddison is one of them. As a young boy, he was one of the fastest amateur racers in Australia, often beating Chad Reed. But by the time he was ready to turn pro, he realized he didn't have the speed to make a comfortable salary, so instead, he focused on **freestyle** motocross. Maddison quickly became Australia's top freestyle rider. Soon, he was traveling the world doing exciting freestyle competitions. But he also liked jumping his motorcycle far. He learned that he could jump farther than anybody he knew. This made him want to set the world record for the farthest jump. On New Year's Eve 2007, Maddison got his chance in Las Vegas.

The stunt aired on ESPN, live for millions of people to see. Even though it was windy, "Maddo" was determined to attempt the jump. He rode nearly 100 mph (160 km/h) and hit the ramp perfectly. The crowd gasped as Maddison flew 322.5 feet (98.3m), beating the old record by 45 feet (13.7m)!

Who s Next?

From the beginning of the sport, there have always been dominant countries in motocross. That doesn't mean they're the only nations that have produced great riders, though. In fact, motocross is popular the world over. South Africa has produced World Champions and AMA Champions. Finland, Italy, Germany, and even the U.S.S.R. have also had moments of championship glory. And many countries that have had limited global success have their own exciting national circuits. From Canada to Japan, from Mexico to Iceland, and from China to Jamaica — anywhere there's dirt, you'll probably find motocross.

Aussie Robbie Maddison has been known to jump (and flip) over some pretty crazy things.

Maddison currently holds three world records for distance jumping.

Glossary

AMA American Motocross Association, the organization that runs motocross racing in North America

brand The name of a product made by a specific company

casual Easygoing, informal

endorsements Agreements between athletes and companies that pay the athletes for promoting the companies' products

freestyle A form of motocross where riders perform jumps and stunts

heroic Brave, bold, daring

modest Quiet and laid-back; not boastful

Nordic Coming from countries such as Norway and Sweden

pastime A hobby

patriotic To support one's country

podium A small platform where winners receive their prizes

prestigious Highly regarded, well known

scarce Rare, hard to find

specialist A person who is an expert in a small area of interest

stamina The ability to do something well over a long period of time

tendency Doing something similar over and over again

Index

Aberg, Bengt 12
AMA Motocross Championships 4, 20, 21, 22, 23

Bayle, Jean-Michel 24, 25
Belgium 4, 6, 16, 17
Bercy Supercross 27

Carlqvist, Hakan 15
Carmichael, Ricky 17, 23
Coppins, Josh 30

DeCoster, Roger 16, 17
Dobb, James 10
Dye, Edison 14

Everts, Stefan 18, 19

France 6, 24, 25, 26, 27

Grand Prix 4, 9
Great Britain 4, 6, 8, 9, 10, 11

Hallman, Torsten 12, 14
Hannah, Bob "Hurricane" 20, 21
Hansson, Marcus 15
Hudson, Neil 10
Husqvarna 14

KTM 18

Lines, Harold 8
Lundin, Sten 12

Maddison, Robbie "Maddo" 30, 31
McGrath, Jeremy 22

Motocross of Nations 4, 5, 6, 7, 9, 10, 17, 18, 21

Netherlands 5
Nilsson, Bill 12, 13
Noyce, Graham 10

Peter Chamberlain Trophy 7
Pourcel, Christophe 26

Ramon, Steve 19
Ray, Bob 8
Reed, Chad 28, 29
Roncada, Stephen 26

Searle, Tommy 11
Smith, Jeff 9
Smith, Marty 20, 21

Stocker, Jack 8
Sweden 12, 13, 14, 15

Team Suzuki 17
Thorpe, Daryl 10
Tibblin, Rolf 12
Townley, Ben 30

United States 20, 21, 22, 23

Vimond, Jacky 24
Vuillemin, David 26

Ward, Geoff 8
World Championships 4, 8, 9, 10, 12, 15

X Games 22

32